Wee Chee Chee

Wee Chee Chee

Written by

Mary Ford

Illustrated by

Chuck Gilmore

Edited by

Corrie Karnan

ISBN -10: 1984264206
ISBN-13: 978-1984264206

DEDICATION

The story of *Wee Chee Chee* is dedicated to my late Great Aunt Mary Ford and my Father Chuck Gilmore who illustrated the book. Chuck was Aunt Mary's nephew.

Mary Ford was born August 3, 1901 and passed April 23, 1980. Chuck Gilmore was born November 14, 1922 and passed July 30, 2008.

ACKNOWLEDGMENTS

In the early 1950's Great Aunt Mary Ford wrote the story of *Wee Chee Chee*. The story would have been lost forever if it wasn't for a joint effort of the Gilmore family.

My first cousin Rich Gilmore found and stored the original story after Mary Ford's death.

Marsha (Gilmore) Henry, Corrie (Gilmore) Karnan and Doug Gilmore, the children of Chuck Gilmore, remembered the story of *Wee Chee Chee* from childhood. We recalled the times our father Chuck Gilmore illustrated the story and Great Aunt Mary read her story to us in the 1960's.

Rachel (Gilmore) Annett, the daughter of Doug Gilmore, computerized and restored the pictures used in the story.

Wee Chee Chee

Sleeka

Skipper

Scamper

Mother Squirrel

Wee Chee Chee

It was very early in the morning and everything was quiet.

Mother Squirrel and her four little squirrels were sleeping in their hollow tree home in the big old oak tree.

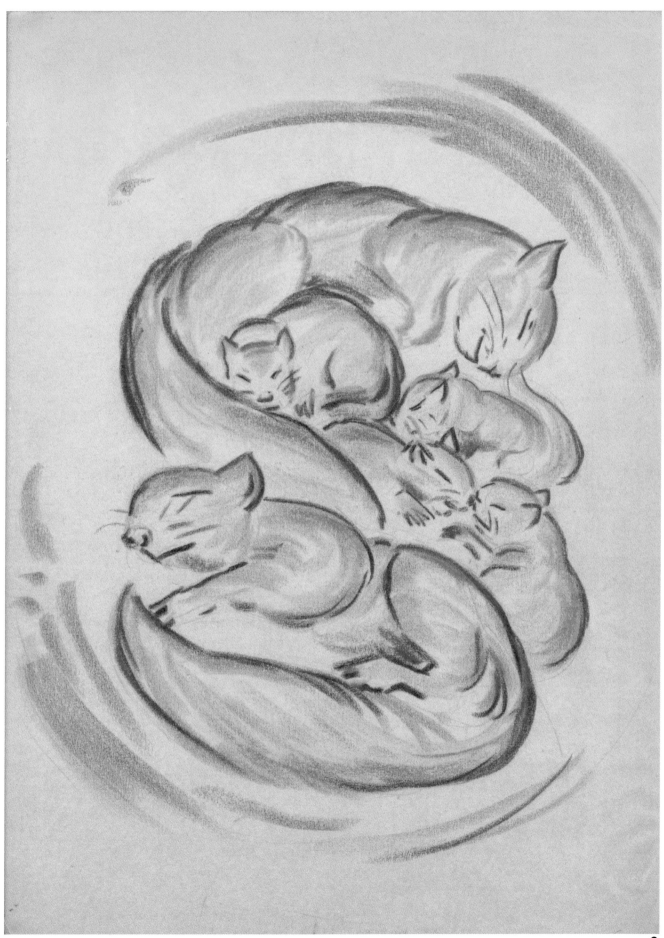

A terrible big noise awakened Mother Squirrel.

She sat up on her hind feet and listened in the hollow of the tree. She ran up to the hole in the side of the tree and looked out.

The sun shone through the quiet branches of the trees.

Father Robin was sitting on a limb above the nest where Mother Robin sat on top of their baby birds.

Mother Squirrel wanted to talk to Father Robin about the big noise, but she was afraid to go very far away from the door of her home in the hollow of their tree.

She turned her head on one side and listened carefully. She couldn't hear a sound. She couldn't even hear the birds singing.

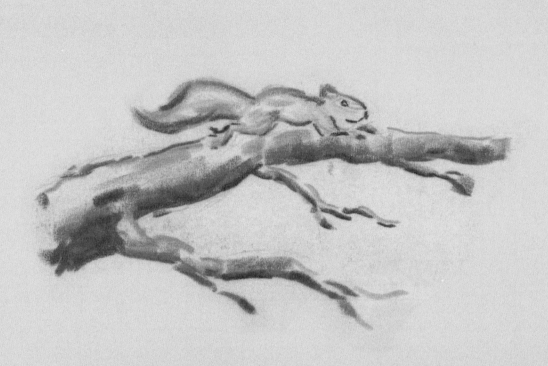

Mother Squirrel climbed out of the hollow through the hole, looked around, then she ran quietly along the limb of the old oak tree, up to Father Robin.

She stood up on her hind feet and leaned over close to Father Robin and whispered.

"Did you hear that terrible big noise?"

"Yes, I heard it," chirped Father Robin quietly, right into Mother Squirrel's ear.

"Do you know what it was?" Mother Squirrel whispered, still standing very close to Father Robin.

"No, and I can't imagine what it was!" he chirped. "I am going to stay near Mother Robin and our babies."

When Mother Squirrel came back, Wee Chee Chee, the biggest little squirrel, was waiting for her right inside the hole of their tree.

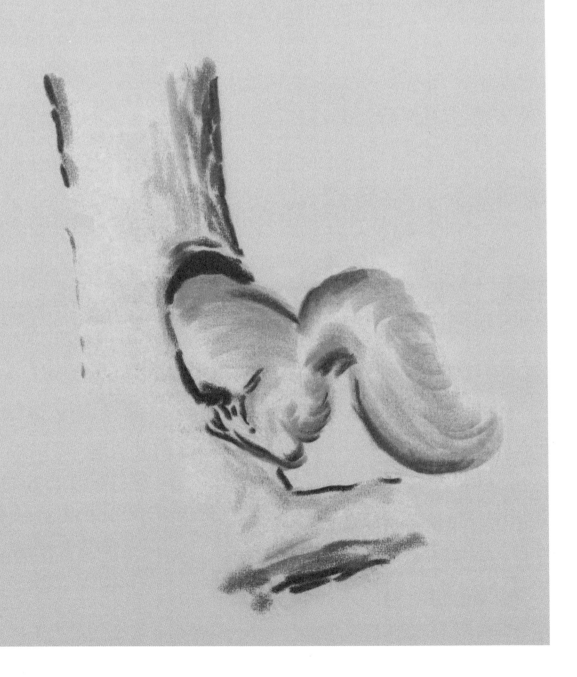

"Wee Chee Chee," Mother Squirrel said in an excited voice.

"Father Robin and I heard a terrible big noise this morning. We don't know what it was. I think we had better move over to the tall maple tree right away. Something might happen to you little squirrels here. I will go now and build our summer home. Then I will come back and get you and the other little squirrels. All of you must stay inside of our home."

Then Mother Squirrel frisked her big, brown, bushy tail and ran out onto a limb.

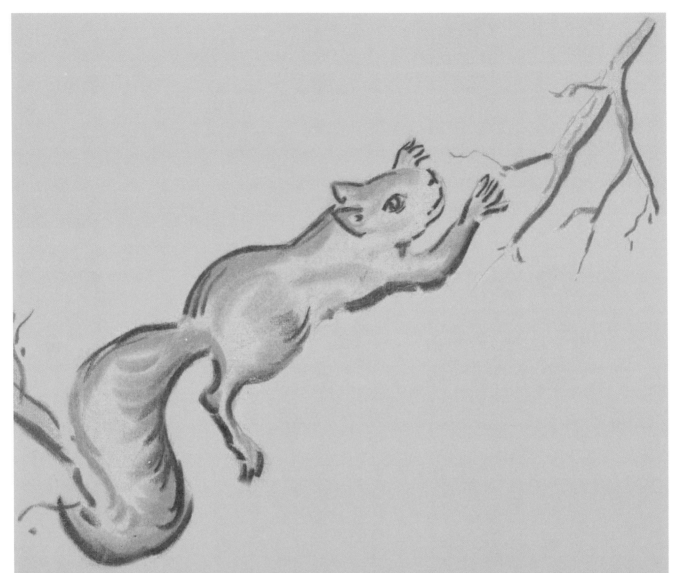

Quickly she went running and jumping through the branches of the old oak tree to the other oak tree, next door. She ran through its branches and jumped across to the tall maple tree. She found a good place for their new summer home and began cutting small branches for it. She put the branches together very carefully. When Mother Squirrel had finished, she went back to their home in the old oak tree.

Right after breakfast, Mother Squirrel took her four little squirrels up to the hole in the side of their tree home. Wee Chee Chee was the prettiest and sleekest of the four little squirrels. Scamper and Skipper were the two little brother squirrels and Sleeka was the cute little sister squirrel.

Mother Squirrel took the little squirrels out onto a big limb and helped them wash their faces with their paws. Then she helped them comb their fur and tails with their teeth.

Wee Chee Chee had already learned how to do this. He washed his face and his ears very well with his little front paws. He washed his soft brown coat all over with his little pink tongue and combed it all over with his little sharp teeth, round and round to its very end. Then he sat up on his hind feet and frisked his tail.

When the little squirrels were all cleaned up and were sitting on a limb in front of her, Mother Squirrel said.

"Little Squirrels, listen! You must do just as I tell you to do if you are to be safe as we go to the tall maple tree!"

"I will carry you one at a time. You must be very quiet as I run and jump through the branches of the trees with you. When I put you down on a limb of the new tree, you must stay right there and wait for me!"

"Wee Chee Chee, I will take you first," said Mother Squirrel.

"Chee Chee Chee!" cried Wee Chee Chee. Then, squealing a loud squeal that frightened the other little squirrels, he turned a quick flip-flop right there on that limb. He almost knocked Scamper off as he came down.

"I'll be a good squirrel, Mother!" He exclaimed. "And you can depend on me to stay on that limb in the new tree!"

Mother Squirrel looked at the other little squirrels and said, "Scamper, Skipper, and Sleeka, you stay here until I come back."

Mother Squirrel picked Wee Chee Chee up in her mouth, as mother squirrels do, and Wee Chee Chee wrapped himself around his mother's neck, as little squirrels do.

Then Mother Squirrel ran up the side of the old tree and out onto a big branch that grew toward the other oak tree next door, carrying Wee Chee Chee in her mouth. He was so excited!

Mother Squirrel ran quickly along the big branch to its very end - then - she stopped.

Wee Chee Chee knew that she was getting ready to jump into the green leafy branches of the other oak tree. He hoped she would make it - and he was pretty sure that she would.

He lay closer to her neck on both sides. Just then Mother Squirrel's feet left the branch and she and Wee Chee Chee were going through the air!

Wee Chee Chee shut his little squirrel eyes and held his little squirrel breath. He had no time to think what might happen if they should drop to the ground. He felt a branch sway, up and down, under them. Mother Squirrel had made it!

He opened his eyes and looked at the blue sky above them as his mother continued to ran on through the branches.

Wee Chee Chee was safely inside his Mother's mouth.

Suddenly Wee Chee Chee heard a little voice way down below them say,

"Hi, there, Wee Chee Chee! Where are you and your mother going?"

It was Romper, the little rabbit. In the past they had played together on the ground.

Wee Chee Chee wanted to call down to him and tell him that he was going to live in the maple tree, but he remembered his mother had told him that he must be quiet. So, he didn't say one word.

Maybe Romper would follow them along on the ground as Wee Chee Chee and his mother were traveling above through the trees.

Suddenly Father Robin flew by Mother Squirrel and Wee Chee Chee.

"That big noise was a land-slide. It's over now. We're all safe," he said. "Nothing will harm the little squirrels!"

Mother Squirrel frisked her bushy, brown tail as if to say, "Thank you, Father Robin!" With Wee Chee Chee still in her mouth, Mother squirrel ran on toward the tall maple tree knowing they would like living there.

"Come back to the old oak tree and see me, Wee Chee Chee!" called Father Robin.

Wee Chee Chee wanted to tell him to come to the maple tree, but he knew that he should be quiet, so he didn't say one word.

The jump that Mother Squirrel had to make to the tall maple tree was so big that Wee Chee Chee shut his little squirrel eyes and held his little squirrel breath again - but Mother Squirrel had made it!

When Wee Chee Chee opened his eyes,
Mother Squirrel was running along a big limb.
Pretty soon she sat him down on it.

"Wee Chee Chee," she said in the kindest
Mother Squirrel voice he had ever heard.

"You stay right here until I come back with the
other little squirrels".

And then in the sweetest little squirrel voice Mother Squirrel had ever heard, Wee Chee Chee said,

"I will stay right here, Mother." Then he rubbed his little nose against his mother's nose.

Wee Chee Chee watched his mother run out on the limb and disappear into the heavy branches. Then he looked around in the tall maple tree. He was so glad to be there - it was so cool and quiet.

Suddenly he felt so tired and sleepy - so tired and sleepy that he didn't even hear Romper, down under the maple tree, call up to him.

"Wee Chee Chee, I'm here!"

Wee Chee Chee had stretched out on the limb and gone to sleep.

He dreamed of playing in the branches of the tall maple tree with Scamper, Skipper and little Sleeka. Mother Squirrel watched, Father Robin sang, and Romper danced below.

The End

ABOUT THE AUTHOR

Mary Ford was a teacher in a one room school house in Fairbury, Nebraska which is south of Lincoln, Nebraska. As a teacher in the 40's and 50's she was always striving to find or create literature using phonics and vocabulary along with inspiring and captivating illustrations for her students to learn to read and write. *Wee Chee Chee* came from her love of animals, her sense of play and her desire to give as much as she could to her students. Mary did have one great fear and that was a fear that a Copyright would not protect her dear *Wee Chee Chee* from theft of her work. As a result Mary never did follow through with getting her book published when she was alive even though the entire family encouraged her to publish. The manuscript, on plain lined paper, was shoved in a drawer, put in the garage, covered in tossed out items and trash until it was taken to be stored by the family after her death.

Made in the USA
Middletown, DE
25 October 2020